A FIRST BOOK OF ACTION PLAYS FOR YOU TO FINISH

ANN FARQUHAR-SMITH

HULTON EDUCATIONAL
PUBLICATIONS

© 1978
Ann Farquhar-Smith

ISBN 0 7175 0804 8

By the same author:
EIGHT PLAYS TO FINISH
MORE PLAYS TO FINISH
PROBLEM PLAYS

First published 1978 by Hulton Educational Publications Ltd.,
Raans Road, Amersham, Bucks.
Printed and bound in Great Britain at
The Camelot Press Ltd, Southampton

CONTENTS

FOREWORD

These ten plays have been written with short, simple lines that are easily read by primary and middle school children of average reading ability. The characters are uncomplicated, with well-defined roles which pupils will enjoy interpreting. The action of each play proceeds at a pace which will maintain the interest of the class, whether they are actors or audience.

The author has not concluded her plays, but taken each to an exciting point and suspended the action – a true cliff-hanger, and literally so in one play! Children are asked to use their imagination to invent a plausible ending, and having acted out the first part of the play they should have no difficulty in extemporising and finding an ingenious dénouement. One or two possible approaches are briefly outlined.

It is hoped that these plays, with their modern idiom and up-to-date themes, will encourage the enjoyment of drama at an age when children are, perhaps, least self-conscious and most keen to participate. They may also benefit in other ways – in the improvement of reading skills, in the development of acting talent and self-expression and in the creation of new ideas and dialogue.

GOING UP!

*

Characters

SIMON
ALI
SUSAN
KATE KING
MRS. KING, who is rather hysterical
MR. LONG, who doesn't like children
MRS. HILTON, who's always moaning

Going Up!

The hallway on the ground floor of Blox flats

SIMON: Come on, lift! I bet it's got stuck again.

SUSAN: Someone's left the door open, I'll bet.

SIMON: I'll try ringing again.

MR. LONG: Leave that button alone. It won't do any good pressing it over and over again.

MRS. HILTON: I don't think those kids should be allowed to use the lifts.

MR. LONG: That's right. Their young legs can get them to the top, no trouble at all.

ALI: Twenty storeys! Come off it, mister. My young legs would be old by the time I got up there.

MRS. KING: I don't know why the council had to put us here in the first place. I hate heights.

KATE: Oh, Mum, don't complain. It's better than our old house. We didn't even have hot water there!

MRS. KING: But I *could* see the ground when I looked out of the window.

SUSAN: Here's the lift now.

SIMON: And about time, too.

ALI: There's nobody in it.

MR. LONG: Well there is now. I'm in it. Are you kids coming?

KATE: Come on, Mum.

MRS. KING: Don't push me, Kate, I'm coming into the horrible thing.

MRS. HILTON: Well hurry up, then. We haven't got all day.

MR. LONG: What floors do you want?

SUSAN: Sixteenth!

MRS. KING: Twelfth!

MRS. HILTON: Sixth!

MR. LONG: And the fifteenth for me. Right – sixteenth, twelfth, sixth.

MRS. KING: No I don't. I promised to drop off a loaf of bread to Mrs. Price. She's on the eleventh.

MR. LONG: Make up your mind, woman. I'm not the lift boy, you know.

ALI: Nobody asked you to press the buttons.

SIMON: Oh, leave him, Ali. It's the only excitement he gets in the day.

MRS. KING: I hate these things. My legs feel all wobbly.

KATE: Don't worry, Mum. We'll be there in a minute.

MR. LONG: We've stopped.

SIMON: Of course we've stopped. We're not going up.

SUSAN: Who wanted the sixth floor?

MRS. HILTON: This isn't the sixth floor. We're only at the third floor.

ALI: Someone's called the lift, of course.

MR. LONG: Then why haven't they come in?

SUSAN: Maybe they want to go down and we're going up.

SIMON: They'd have to be very thin to get on this lift.

MR. LONG: What do you mean?

SIMON: Look out of the little window. We're not at a floor. We're stuck between two floors.

MRS. KING: Help! We're stuck! Help! Let me out of here!

MR. LONG: Now calm down. Let's see. What do we want? Emergency brake.

ALI: I don't think we're going to need that. We're well and truly stopped.

MR. LONG: All right – emergency bell. I'll press that.

MRS. KING: And who's going to hear that? I tell you, we're trapped!

KATE: Oh, Mum, give it up. It's all right. Don't panic.

MRS. HILTON: Somebody must hear that bell. It's loud enough to wake the dead.

SUSAN: But not the caretaker. I just remembered – he went out in his car, just as we came into the flats.

MRS. KING: Oh no! We'll all die of thirst. Help! I've got to get out of here.

KATE: Quiet, Mum – don't worry. It'll be all right. You'll see.

MR. LONG: It's you kids that are to blame. Monkeying about in the lifts. Joy-riding up and down from morning till night.

SUSAN: It isn't us – it's the kids from the other blocks that muck about.

MRS. KING: Get me out of here!

KATE: We've done all we can. We'll just have to wait now.

MRS. KING: I can't wait. I've got to get out of here.

SIMON: O.K. Out you go. There's the escape hatch in the roof.

MRS. KING: I couldn't get up there! Just get me out of here!

MR. LONG: Now calm down. It won't do any good getting over-excited.

MRS. HILTON: I remember reading about some people who were stuck in a lift once. They were there for hours before anyone found them.

MRS. KING: Oh, no! I can't stand it.

SIMON: Then sit down.

SUSAN: This isn't getting us anywhere.

ALI: Neither is the lift.

SIMON: If the caretaker's gone out, then who is going to hear the bell?

MRS. KING: Nobody will hear it! We'll all die!

KATE: Please, Mum, try to get a grip on yourself.

SIMON: What about the emergency telephone?

MR. LONG: What telephone? Oh yes, I'd forgotten about that. Hello! Hello!

MRS. HILTON: Isn't that connected to the caretaker's flat as well?

SUSAN: And he's gone out.

MRS. LONG: Maybe there's some way of switching it over when he goes out.

SIMON: And maybe there's not.

ALI: Or maybe he forgot.

MR. LONG: There's one thing that's certain. There's no reply.

MRS. HILTON: What about the escape hatch, then?

MR. LONG: Look at it. It's far too small to get through.

MRS. HILTON: You're right. Only a midget could get through there.

SUSAN: Or a child.

MR. LONG: What are you talking about?

SIMON: She's right. One of us could get through there.

ALI: And then what? Climb up the cable? Even if we could, how could we open the door from the inside?

SIMON: If there's someone waiting for the lift there, they could help. They'd see you through the glass.

ALI: Wait a minute. I never said that I would go.

MRS. KING: My Kate can't go. Don't leave me, Kate.

KATE: Don't worry, Mum. I couldn't do it.

SUSAN: Don't look at me. I can't even climb a rope – I'm hopeless at P.E.

SIMON: It's a toss-up between us two, then.

ALI: I don't want to go. I'm a coward from way back.

SIMON: So am I. That makes two of us and that's why we'll have to toss for it.

SUSAN: Are you sure you should even try?

MRS. HILTON: You might be killed.

MRS. KING: If one of them doesn't go, we'll all die!

MR. LONG: There isn't much danger really. The gap between the floors isn't much at all. You might even find that the top of the lift is level with the bottom of the doors.

SIMON: Don't look at me like that, mister. We haven't even tossed yet.

ALI: Heads you win, tails I lose!

SIMON: Come off it! I wasn't born yesterday.

MR. LONG: I'll toss the coin. Who calls?

ALI/SIMON: I will.

MR. LONG: You call, then.

SIMON: O.K. Heads!

MR. LONG: Heads it is. That means the other lad goes.

ALI: I knew this was going to be my lucky day!

SIMON: How are you going to get up to the escape hatch?

ALI: Good point. Sorry everyone, I can't reach.

MR. LONG: I'll give you a leg up.

ALI: I knew I couldn't get away with it.

MR. LONG: Put your foot here and up you go.

ALI: I can't move the escape hatch.

MRS. HILTON: Keep trying.

MR. LONG: Sorry, lad. I can't hold you any more.

ALI: Ouch! O.K., you can't say I didn't try.

MRS. KING: Oh, no! Get me out of here.

MR. LONG: Come on. If at first you don't succeed . . .

ALI: Give up.

MR. LONG: That's what's wrong with youngsters today. They've got no guts. Up you go again and try pushing it upwards this time.

ALI: That's what I was doing last time.

SIMON: Push it sideways, then.

ALI: There it goes.

MRS. HILTON: Ugh! What a lot of dust.

MR. LONG: Down you come again, lad.

ALI: I think I can get near enough to pull myself through.

MR. LONG: Ready, then. Up you go again.

ALI: Here goes!

SIMON: He's made it. Are you all right, Ali?

ALI: Yes, we're almost up to the next floor. I'll try and reach the glass panel on the door.

MR. LONG: Can you see anyone standing there?

ALI: I don't think so.

SIMON: Hey! Help! The lift's started to move again.

NOW YOU CAN FINISH THE PLAY YOURSELVES

Here are some ideas for finishing the play:

1 What happens to Ali when the lift moves?
2 Why has the lift started to move?
3 Is the lift going up or down?
4 What should the people in the lift do to help Ali?

THE FOOTBALL POOLS

*

Characters

MR. WESTON
MRS. WESTON
ALICE WESTON
MAURICE WESTON
OLIVER, his friend
VOICE ON TELEVISION

The Football Pools

The action of the play takes place in the Westons' living-room on a Saturday evening

VOICE: Aston Villa, two, Sunderland, two.

MR. WESTON: That's another one!

MRS. WESTON: Another what, dear?

MR. WESTON: Another draw! Sh!

(Maurice Weston and Oliver come in.)

MAURICE: Have you seen my green anorak, Mum?

MR. WESTON: Sh! Maurice. I'm trying to check my pools.

MRS. WESTON: No, I haven't seen it, dear.

OLIVER: I told you. You must have left it at school.

MAURICE: I couldn't have left it at school. I was wearing it on Friday.

MRS. WESTON: No you weren't, dear. You had to wear your best jacket to school on Friday.

MR. WESTON: Will you please be quiet? I've got five draws already.

OLIVER: Well done, Mr. Weston. How did Leeds get on?

MR. WESTON: I don't know. I'm only interested in draws.

MRS. WESTON: You really must try to be more careful with your things, Maurice.

VOICE: Luton nought . . .

MR. WESTON: Now that's torn it!

MRS. WESTON: What's wrong now, dear?

MR. WESTON: Something's wrong with the sound on the telly. Switch on the radio.

MRS. WESTON: It's in the kitchen. I'll go and get it.

(Mrs. Weston goes out.)

MR. WESTON: Well, hurry up. I don't want to miss the rest of the results.

OLIVER: Come on, Maurice. Let's go out.

MAURICE: I can't go out until I find my anorak.

(Mrs. Weston comes in.)

MRS. WESTON: The radio isn't in the kitchen. Oh, I remember now, Alice took it up to her room.

MR. WESTON: Well, go and get it, then! Why must I be surrounded by fools?

MAURICE: That's because you're always surrounded by your family.

MRS. WESTON: I can't go up to Alice's room. She's got her boy friend in there.

MR. WESTON: I don't care if she's got the Prime Minister in there! Get me that radio.

MRS. WESTON: *(Shouts)*: Alice! Alice! Bring me down the radio, please.

ALICE *(Off)*: What did you say, Mum? I can't hear you.

MAURICE: Of course she can't hear you. She's listening to the radio.

MR. WESTON: Less of your cheek, Maurice, or you'll get a thick ear.

MRS. WESTON *(Shouts)*: Bring the radio down, dear.

OLIVER: I'll go up and get it for you, Mr. Weston.

(Oliver goes out.)

MRS. WESTON: That's very kind of Oliver, isn't it?

MR. WESTON: This telly's really had its day. And for it to pack up now, of all times.

(Oliver comes in.)

OLIVER: Here you are, Mr. Weston.

MR. WESTON: Thank you, Oliver. I bet it's tuned to some awful programme of pop music.

MAURICE: I don't think that Alice would be listening to the football results.

MR. WESTON: Quiet, Maurice, while I find the right station.

VOICE: Scottish League Premier Division . . .

MR. WESTON: I've missed the Fourth Division.

VOICE: Aberdeen, one, Celtic, one.

MR. WESTON: I've got another draw!

MRS. WESTON: Is that good, dear? Are we going to win?

(Alice comes in.)

ALICE: Hey, Dad, give me back my radio.

MR. WESTON: Leave that radio alone!

ALICE: It's not your radio. I bought it out of my wages.

MR. WESTON: Leave that radio alone. This is my house, and I'll say who listens to the radio in it.

MRS. WESTON: Just humour your father, Alice. We may win the pools this week!

ALICE: He's been saying that for as long as I can remember.

MR. WESTON: You can have your radio back in a minute. Just let me listen to the rest of the results.

ALICE: Oh, all right. I'll have ten per cent of your winnings, though.

MR. WESTON: You can have fifty per cent if you leave me in peace.

ALICE: You all heard that, didn't you?

VOICE: Clydebank versus Morton, late kick-off.

MR. WESTON: Oh no, I might need that one.

MRS. WESTON: Well, you'll have to be patient, dear.

ALICE: I'm not lending you my radio for half the night.

MR. WESTON: All right. I'm nearly finished.

VOICE: And that is the end of the football results. The pools forecast is very good. Telegram claims are required for twenty-four points.

MR. WESTON: If I only had those Fourth Division results!

MAURICE: We'll go out and get you a paper, Dad.

MR. WESTON: Will you? That's very good of you, Maurice. Here's the money, and hurry back.

(Oliver and Maurice go out.)

ALICE: And I'll take this back up to my room.

(Alice goes out.)

MR. WESTON: All right. That last result will probably be on the telly.

MRS. WESTON: At least we'll be able to see it, even if we can't hear it.

MR. WESTON: Well, Ada. This might be it! The big one at last!

MRS. WESTON: What do you mean, Sid?

MR. WESTON: I've got seven draws so far. If I get one more draw, we'll have twenty-four points – especially on the system I use.

MRS. WESTON: I can't believe it, Sid. We've never won anything!

MR. WESTON: Keep your fingers crossed, Ada. We'll know when the boys bring the paper back.

MRS. WESTON: Just think of it, Sid. All that money!

MR. WESTON: A new house. A new car.

MRS. WESTON: New clothes. A holiday somewhere in the sun.

MR. WESTON: A new telly!

MRS. WESTON: No more worrying about money.

MR. WESTON: No more work. I can tell old Law exactly what he can do with his mouldy old office.

MRS. WESTON: You won't have to get up and catch the train every morning. Oh Sid, it's too good to be true.

MR. WESTON: It probably is, too. I won't have that Fourth Division draw.

MRS. WESTON: Look, here's a result now. Is that the one you want?

MR. WESTON: Two-one. Just my luck; that's no good at all. It all stands on the Fourth Division now. Where is that boy with the paper?

MRS. WESTON: I do hope he hurries back. He's been so absent-minded recently. What with losing his anorak and things.

MR. WESTON: I'll have to speak to him sharply about pulling his socks up. We can't let him go on like this.

(Maurice and Oliver come in.)

MAURICE: Here you are, Dad. They'd just arrived at the shop as we got there.

MR. WESTON: Right. Fourth Division. Of course, they're all in the smudgy "Stop Press". Scunthorpe. That's what I'm looking for. It's a draw! I've done it. I've got eight draws.

MRS. WESTON: I can't believe it, Sid.

OLIVER: This is your lucky day. We met my Mum on the way.

MAURICE: And she's found my anorak.

OLIVER: Maurice left it at my house on Thursday night.

MR. WESTON: What a time to talk about anoraks. It's mink coats we should be talking about.

MAURICE: I forgot all about going to Oliver's on Thursday night. I was on my way to . . .

MRS. WESTON: What's wrong, Maurice?

MR. WESTON: The boy's gone an awful colour. Are you all right, son?

MRS. WESTON: Maurice, what's wrong with you? Why have you got your hand in your anorak pocket?

MAURICE: I was on the way to post Dad's pools coupon. I forgot! It's still here in my pocket!

NOW YOU CAN FINISH THE PLAY YOURSELVES

Here are some ideas for finishing the play:

1 Has Maurice really forgotten to post the coupon?
2 If he has, what will his parents say?
3 If he hasn't, and the coupon has been posted, what will they do with the money?
4 If they have won, will Alice really demand her fifty per cent?

THE SAFARI PARK

*

Characters

MR. FLEMING
MRS. FLEMING
LEE FLEMING
DONNA FLEMING
FIRST WARDEN
SECOND WARDEN
MONKEY

The Safari Park

The action of the play takes place in the Flemings' car as they drive through the Safari Park

MR. FLEMING: Blimey! I only want a ticket. I don't want to buy the whole park!

MRS. FLEMING: Pay the man, Fred. There's a queue of cars behind us.

LEE: Come on, Dad. You can't back out now.

DONNA: You promised.

MR. FLEMING: I didn't think it was going to bankrupt me.

MRS. FLEMING: It *is* a special treat.

MR. FLEMING: All right. Here are the tickets. Are you satisfied? Daylight robbery.

DONNA: Oooh! What was that?

LEE: It's a cattle grid. It keeps the animals in.

DONNA: And the people out.

LEE: I'm hungry, Mum.

MRS. FLEMING: You can't be hungry, Lee. It's only an hour since you had your dinner.

DONNA: He's always hungry. That's why he's so fat.

LEE: I'm not fat, I'm just well built.

DONNA: Yes you are. Fatty! Fatty!

MR. FLEMING: If you two won't stop fighting, I'll stop this car and we'll go right home.

LEE: Sorry! I'll be good if you give me some crisps.

MRS. FLEMING: I shouldn't really, but here you are.

DONNA: It *is* hot in here. Can I open a window?

MR. FLEMING: I should think so. It's only when we get to the lions that we have to keep them shut.

LEE: Look at that monkey!

DONNA: Looks just like you, Lee!

MR. FLEMING: I won't tell you again.

DONNA: Sorry Dad, honest.

LEE: Do you think he'd like a crisp?

MRS. FLEMING: You know you're not allowed to feed the animals.

LEE: One little crisp won't hurt.

DONNA: Here he comes.

LEE: Come on, little monkey – have a crisp.

MRS. FLEMING: Look out! He's coming in the window.

(Monkey comes in.)

MRS. FLEMING: Get him out, get him out!

MR. FLEMING: I can't get him out. I've got to drive. You get him out.

LEE: He's pinched my crisps!

DONNA: He's pulling my hair. Get off!

MRS. FLEMING: Look what he's done to my dress! Fred! Fred! Do something!

LEE: I can't catch him. Ouch! He's bitten me!

MR. FLEMING: Now he's on my lap. I can't see where I'm going.

MRS. FLEMING: Stop pressing the horn. You'll scare all the animals.

MR. FLEMING: It's not me. It's this blooming monkey.

LEE: Here comes the warden's jeep.

MRS. FLEMING: Thank goodness. Call him over, Fred.

DONNA: He's coming, anyway.

(First Warden comes in.)

WARDEN: Good afternoon. Would you please not sound your horn in the park, sir.

MR. FLEMING: I'm not sounding the horn.

LEE: The monkey is.

WARDEN: You're not allowed to bring your pets in here, sir.

DONNA: We didn't bring him in. He's one of yours.

WARDEN: I see. You're trying to pinch him, are you?

MRS. FLEMING: He's attacking us!

WARDEN: Were you giving him something to eat?

MRS. FLEMING: It wasn't me. It was my son!

LEE: I only gave him a crisp.

WARDEN: Then where did he get that sandwich from?

MRS. FLEMING: Oh NO! He's got at the picnic.

LEE: Bang goes my tea.

WARDEN: All right. I'll take him. Come on, then.

DONNA: Look, the monkey's climbing on to his shoulder.

MR. FLEMING: Thanks a lot.

WARDEN: No trouble, sir. But please, keep the window shut and don't feed the animals.

(First Warden goes out.)

MRS. FLEMING: Am I glad to see the end of that monkey!

DONNA: Well, I don't know if you noticed, but he didn't have a very pretty end!

LEE: That was quite exciting.

DONNA: And painful.

MRS. FLEMING: And smelly.

MR. FLEMING: Phew! You're right. Pity we can't have the window open.

MRS. FLEMING: Then we'll get even more monkeys wrecking the car.

DONNA: Look at the giraffes.

MRS. FLEMING: Don't they look graceful when they run?

LEE: Not like old Jumbo over there. You couldn't call him graceful.

DONNA: No, but he's nice, isn't he?

MRS. FLEMING: Look. He's coming towards us!

MR. FLEMING: Get the camera out. This should make a good picture.

LEE: Here you are, Dad. Lucky the monkey didn't get his hands on it.

MRS. FLEMING: That elephant's coming really close.

DONNA: Maybe he can't see very well. He's got very small eyes for such a big animal.

MRS. FLEMING: Stop the car, Fred! He's coming straight for us.

MR. FLEMING: I have stopped. There. That'll make a good photo. I've never been so close to an elephant before.

MRS. FLEMING: Start the car, Fred. He's going to walk right into us.

MR. FLEMING: Make up your mind, Dora. Stop the car. Start the car. What do you want?

LEE: A new mudguard, I think. Jumbo's just thwacked ours.

DONNA: I'm scared. He's rocking the car.

MRS. FLEMING: He's trying to open the door with his trunk! Stop him, Fred! Stop him!

MR. FLEMING: What do you expect me to do? This isn't in the Highway Code, you know.

LEE: Get an elephant gun from under your seat and shoot him.

DONNA: Have you got to be funny at a time like this?

LEE: All right. I'll start to cry.

MRS. FLEMING: Thank goodness. The warden's here and he's shooing the elephant away.

(Second Warden comes in.)

WARDEN: Are you all right, sir?

MR. FLEMING: I think so, but the car isn't.

WARDEN: Only a little dent, sir. And of course the Safari Park accepts no liability.

DONNA: What does that mean?

LEE: They won't pay for the damage and Dad is about to blow up!

MR. FLEMING: Accept no liability! After all we paid to come in here!

MRS. FLEMING: We've been attacked by a monkey . . .

MR. FLEMING: Had our car wrecked by an elephant . . .

WARDEN: Quiet please, sir. The other clients will be jealous. They're always complaining that the animals are too quiet.

MR. FLEMING: Quiet! These animals are not fit to be near human beings!

MRS. FLEMING: They're only fit for a zoo!

WARDEN: Madam, if you're not prepared to take the risk, you shouldn't come.

MR. FLEMING: All right. Just tell me the shortest way out of here.

WARDEN: Certainly, sir. Straight on, down the road, then take the first left.

MRS. FLEMING: But that'll take us through the lions!

WARDEN: Of course it does, madam. You can't come to the Safari Park and not see the lions. Make sure all your doors and windows are tightly shut.

MR. FLEMING: Don't worry.

WARDEN: And remember to keep to the speed limit in the lions' enclosure. Enjoy your visit.

(Second Warden goes out.)

MR. FLEMING: How does he expect me to enjoy my visit with half the side of the car bashed in?

MRS. FLEMING: And the car smelling of monkey.

LEE: And the picnic pinched.

DONNA: Never mind. We'll be out of here in a moment.

LEE: Take care, Dad. Here are the lions.

DONNA: Don't they look fierce?

MR. FLEMING: Are you sure all the doors and windows are shut?

LEE: Window shut and door locked.

DONNA: Mine too.

MRS. FLEMING: Just as well. That lion's getting close.

DONNA: It's not a lion – it's a lioness.

MRS. FLEMING: Look at the dear little cubs.

LEE: Careful, Dad. That cub's going to run in front of the car.

MR. FLEMING: All right. I can see it.

MRS. FLEMING: That lioness is awfully close now, Fred.

DONNA: She's scratching at the door.

LEE: The door's opening!

MR. FLEMING: It can't be. I locked it myself.

MRS. FLEMING: The elephant must have damaged the lock!

DONNA: The lioness is coming in!

NOW YOU CAN FINISH THE PLAY YOURSELVES

Here are some ideas for finishing the play:

1 Is one of the wardens going to rescue them again?
2 How is he going to go about it?
3 What will the lioness do next?
4 What is the best action the Fleming family can take?

CRASH LANDING

*

Characters

UNCLE JACK
SHARON EVANS
CLYDE EVANS
MRS. EVANS
VOICE IN CONTROL TOWER
CHIEF INSTRUCTOR

Crash Landing

The action of the play takes place inside a small aircraft

MRS. EVANS: It's awfully good of Uncle Jack to take us for a flip like this.

UNCLE JACK: My pleasure, Doris, my pleasure.

CLYDE: Can I sit next to you, please, Uncle Jack?

MRS. EVANS: Will he be all right there in the front, Jack?

UNCLE JACK: Of course he will, Doris.

MRS. EVANS: He won't fall out, will he?

UNCLE JACK: Don't worry, Doris. You'll all be strapped in.

SHARON: Why can't I sit in the front?

CLYDE: I asked first.

UNCLE JACK: We'll do a quick trip. Then I'll land and Sharon can sit in the front for the next trip.

CLYDE: O.K. But I'm first.

SHARON: Just like a boy.

UNCLE JACK: Are you girls comfy there in the back?

MRS. EVANS: Yes thanks, Jack.

SHARON: It's a bit squashed, isn't it?

CLYDE: It's an aeroplane – not a taxi.

UNCLE JACK: Clyde and I did the checks while you girls were in the club house, so we're ready to roll. All seat belts fastened?

MRS. EVANS: Yes, Jack. Sharon and I are both strapped in tight.

UNCLE JACK: Here we go, then. Alpha Lima, permission to take off.

VOICE: Alpha Lima, clear to take off.

UNCLE JACK: Roger. Alpha Lima take off. Hold on to your hats.

SHARON: It's bumpy.

CLYDE: That's the grass.

MRS. EVANS: It's not bumpy any more.

UNCLE JACK: We're airborne. Up we go.

MRS. EVANS: Doesn't everything look little and far away?

SHARON: Look how small the cars are.

CLYDE: The river looks nice from here with the sun shining on it.

UNCLE JACK: We'll do a wide circuit of the airfield, just to show you around.

MRS. EVANS: Rocks about a bit, doesn't it?

UNCLE JACK: You can't help that in an aeroplane this size.

CLYDE: You're not in a Jumbo now, Mum.

UNCLE JACK: Would you like to have a go at the controls, Clyde?

CLYDE: Can I?

MRS EVANS: Is it wise, Jack? After all, he's only a boy.

UNCLE JACK: No problem, Doris. Just hold the stick steady. Push it forward to go down.

CLYDE: Like this?

UNCLE JACK: Steady on. Smoothly does it.

CLYDE: And pull it back to go up.

UNCLE JACK: That's better. Nice and smooth. And to keep it straight and level, there's the trim wheel on your right.

CLYDE: How do you turn the aeroplane?

UNCLE JACK: Move the wheel left and pull slightly to stop it losing height. Can you reach all right?

CLYDE: I can just reach.

UNCLE JACK: Just do what I do.

SHARON: Don't forget us in the back seat!

MRS. EVANS: It may be safe for Clyde to fly, but I wouldn't say it was comfortable.

UNCLE JACK: Now, then. Let's take her up a bit higher.

CLYDE: Can I do it?

UNCLE JACK: Of course. Easy does it. Watch your throttle, too.

CLYDE: Is this the throttle?

UNCLE JACK: That's it. Ouch!

CLYDE: What's the matter, Uncle Jack?

UNCLE JACK: Got a pain *(pant)* in my arm *(pant)*. Oooh!

MRS. EVANS: What's wrong, Jack?

CLYDE: Mum! Uncle Jack's passed out!

SHARON: This is no place to play jokes, Clyde.

CLYDE: I'm not playing jokes. He's gone a funny colour and he's passed out.

MRS. EVANS: Then who's flying the aeroplane?

CLYDE: I am!

SHARON: Oh, no! We'll all be killed.

MRS. EVANS: I knew I should never have come.

CLYDE: Don't panic. I can fly it. Look, I'm keeping it nice and steady.

MRS. EVANS: Lovely! But how are you going to get down?

SHARON: We can't stop up here for ever.

CLYDE: I'll call up the tower and get help.

MRS. EVANS: You don't know how to.

CLYDE: Yes I do. I'll take off Uncle Jack's head-set.

MRS. EVANS: Don't take your hands off the controls.

CLYDE: I'll have to for a minute. Don't worry, I'll set the trim.

MRS. EVANS: Can you reach the head-set? Don't move about too much or we might fall out of the sky.

CLYDE: I've got it. And we can't fall out of the sky as long as I keep it above a certain speed.

SHARON: How do you know?

CLYDE: Never mind. I'll try and call the tower. Alpha Lima calling Woodbridge Tower. May Day, May Day.

MRS. EVANS: What are you talking about? It's August.

SHARON: That's the distress call. Even I know that.

CLYDE: They're not answering. Alpha Lima calling Woodbridge Tower. May Day, May Day.

SHARON: Maybe they've switched off.

CLYDE: Switch! That's it! I have to switch over to get the reply.

VOICE: Woodbridge Tower here. Come in Alpha Lima. What is your emergency? Over.

CLYDE: Alpha Lima here. The pilot has collapsed. There is no one to land the plane. Over.

VOICE: Hello Alpha Lima. Can you identify? How many hours have you got? Over.

CLYDE: I haven't got any hours. I'm a schoolboy. Can you help me? Over.

VOICE: Hello Alpha Lima. Stand by. I have sent for our Chief Instructor. Keep listening while I clear the circuit. Over.

CLYDE: Alpha Lima. Your message received. Over and out.

MRS. EVANS: What's going on?

CLYDE: They've sent for someone to help me land.

SHARON: Why have they stopped talking to you?

CLYDE: Just listen and you'll hear what he's doing.

VOICE: Woodbridge Tower here. We have an emergency. All aircraft clear the runway and circuit. I repeat, all aircraft clear the runway and circuit.

MRS. EVANS: What's all that about?

CLYDE: It means they're getting all the other aircraft out of the way so it's clear for me to try to land.

NOW YOU CAN FINISH THE PLAY YOURSELVES

Here are some ideas for finishing the play:

1 Will Clyde manage to bring the aircraft down safely?
2 How does Mrs. Evans react? Does she hinder Clyde?
3 What does Sharon do?
4 How would you react in the same circumstances — remember, small light aircraft do not carry parachutes!

For this play, here is a possible ending, written with the help of a very experienced pilot.

MRS. EVANS: What's all that about?

CLYDE: It means they're getting all the other aircraft out of the way so it's clear for me to try to land.

CHIEF INSTRUCTOR *(Voice)*: Chief Instructor here. Are you ready to receive me?

CLYDE: Ready and waiting.

CHIEF INSTRUCTOR: If you keep quite calm and do as I say, you should land without any trouble. We have you visual.

SHARON: What does that mean?

CLYDE: He can see us.

CHIEF INSTRUCTOR: Are you flying straight and level? Watch the altimeter. Is it going up or down?

CLYDE: I'm flying pretty straight. I haven't changed anything since Uncle Jack passed out.

CHIEF INSTRUCTOR: Look where the aircraft's nose is on the horizon. Whenever I ask you to fly straight and level, I want you to get that position on the horizon. What's your speed?

CLYDE: One hundred miles an hour.

CHIEF INSTRUCTOR: I'm going to take you all the way out and give you a straight approach.

MRS. EVANS: Why have we got to go far out? Why can't we land right away?

CLYDE: Quiet, Mum.

CHIEF INSTRUCTOR: I can see you. Hold everything steady. I will tell you to turn in about two minutes.

CLYDE: O.K. I'm waiting.

CHIEF INSTRUCTOR: Are you happy about turning?

CLYDE: Yes. Uncle Jack showed me how to turn. He told me to pull back slightly on the wheel.

CHIEF INSTRUCTOR: Good lad. Remember that slight pull back, or you'll lose height in the turn.

CLYDE: When do you want me to close the throttle?

CHIEF INSTRUCTOR: Don't touch anything. I'll bring you in on a straight approach and I'll tell you when to close the throttle.

CLYDE: When do I start turning?

CHIEF INSTRUCTOR: Turn now. I'll tell you when to steady.

CLYDE: I'm turning now.

CHIEF INSTRUCTOR: Steady. Watch the position of the nose. Remember where it was for straight and level flight.

CLYDE: Ooops. Sorry, I didn't pull back enough during the turn.

CHIEF INSTRUCTOR: Can you see the runway on your left now?

CLYDE: Yes, I can. But I'll never get the aircraft down on to such a tiny little strip.

CHIEF INSTRUCTOR: Don't worry. I'll be able to keep you on the line.

CLYDE: What do I do now?

CHIEF INSTRUCTOR: Can you see the master switch?

CLYDE: Yes, I can see it.

CHIEF INSTRUCTOR: Good lad. You're doing fine. As soon as you're on the ground, switch that off.

SHARON: If we ever reach the ground.

CLYDE: O.K. But what do I do NOW?

CHIEF INSTRUCTOR: Turn now.

CLYDE: Turning.

CHIEF INSTRUCTOR: Steady.

CLYDE: Steady she is and we're nicely lined up this time.

CHIEF INSTRUCTOR: You are now. But the wind will drift you off. Don't worry. I'll allow for that. Can you see the flap switch?

CLYDE: Yes. Right here.

CHIEF INSTRUCTOR: Good. Take your hands off the controls. You should still be in trim. Close the throttle now.

CLYDE: What shall I do? The nose has dropped.

CHIEF INSTRUCTOR: Don't touch the controls. Put the flap switch down and keep the nose in that position.

CLYDE: We're coming down nicely now.

CHIEF INSTRUCTOR: It's looking good from here. What is your speed?

CLYDE: Eighty miles per hour.

CHIEF INSTRUCTOR: Keep her coming down. Every time you call me, give me your speed.

CLYDE: Seventy-five miles per hour. When do I start pulling out?

CHIEF INSTRUCTOR: I'll tell you when. Don't worry. Keep her coming down.

CLYDE: Seventy miles per hour. The ground's coming up fast.

CHIEF INSTRUCTOR: Pull the stick back slightly. No. Not that much. Steady. It's looking good. Hold it where it is. Don't move it at all. Switch off the master switch now. Don't worry about the bumps. You've got the whole airfield to stop in.

CLYDE: I think we've landed ten times already.

CHIEF INSTRUCTOR: It wasn't the best landing in history. But you are down in one piece.

UNCLE JACK: Oooh! Where am I?

MRS. EVANS: You're on the ground, Jack. How are you feeling?

UNCLE JACK: A bit groggy. I don't know what came over me.

SHARON: Clyde landed the plane.

UNCLE JACK: He what?

CLYDE: That's right, Uncle Jack. I landed the plane.

SHARON: With a little bit of help, of course. Isn't he super?

CLYDE: Help!

CHIEF INSTRUCTOR: What's the matter? There's a doctor on the way over now.

CLYDE: Nothing's the matter, really. My sister's just kissed me. That's the worst thing that's happened to me today!

TRIP ROUND THE BAY

*

Characters

LEE ALEXANDER
BECKY ALEXANDER
MR. ALEXANDER
JASON JOHNSON
ALISON JOHNSON
MRS. JOHNSON

Trip Round the Bay

The play takes place on board Mr. Alexander's boat, the "Merry May"

MR. ALEXANDER: All aboard, then.

MRS. JOHNSON: I must say, I don't like the look of that cloud.

MR. ALEXANDER: Come on, Mrs. Johnson – it's only a little cloud.

MRS. JOHNSON: Well, I just don't like the look of it, that's all.

JASON: Have you checked the weather forecast, Mr. Alexander?

MR. ALEXANDER: Weather forecast? Who needs them?

LEE: Dad never bothers with them.

BECKY: Says he can feel a storm coming in his bones.

MRS. JOHNSON: Have we got life-jackets?

LEE: I don't think we have enough to go round.

BECKY: We've only got four.

MR. ALEXANDER: Life-jackets! Weather forecasts! We're going for a trip round the bay – not the Fastnet Race.

MRS. JOHNSON: All the same, I'd feel happier if I had a life-jacket.

MR. ALEXANDER: Take mine, Mrs. Johnson.

MRS. JOHNSON: Thanks very much. You see, I can't swim.

MR. ALEXANDER: Everyone ready to cast off, Lee?

LEE: All ready, Dad.

MR. ALEXANDER: Everyone happy? Off we go.

LEE: Cast off now, Dad.

MR. ALEXANDER: Good lad.

MRS. JOHNSON: Be careful, Lee, you're leaning a bit far out.

ALISON: Do stop fussing, Mum. I'm sure Lee can take care of himself.

BECKY: We can always pull him out with a boat-hook.

MRS. JOHNSON: I still don't like the look of that cloud.

JASON: Mum's right. I think the wind's getting up a bit.

MR. ALEXANDER: Nonsense, that's just the sea breeze. You'll really begin to feel it once we leave the harbour.

MRS. JOHNSON: Look at the white horses. Oh dear, I think it's going to be too rough for me.

ALISON: For goodness' sake, Mum – this was supposed to be a treat.

MR. ALEXANDER: Don't worry, Mrs. Johnson. We've been out in a lot worse than this.

MRS. JOHNSON: But I haven't. So please, if it's all the same to you, take me back home.

MR. ALEXANDER: Just wait a minute, Mrs. Johnson. You'll soon be enjoying yourself.

MRS. JOHNSON: I'll only enjoy myself when I can get back to dry land.

ALISON: Come on, Mum, it won't last long.

MRS. JOHNSON: By the look of those waves, we won't last long. We'll capsize any minute now.

MRS. ALEXANDER: All right, Mrs. Johnson, just to make you happy, we'll turn round right now.

JASON: Oh, Mum! Trust you to spoil everything.

MR. ALEXANDER: That's funny?

LEE: What's funny, Dad?

MR. ALEXANDER: The steering. I can't get her to turn round.

LEE: Maybe we've picked up a bit of seaweed on the rudder.

BECKY: Try throwing it about a bit. That might free it.

MRS. JOHNSON: We're being thrown about enough at the moment.

ALISON: But Mr. Alexander's got to try to free the rudder, or we'll never get back home.

MRS JOHNSON: Oooh! I don't feel well.

JASON: Quiet, Mum. You can't be sick here. It's not our boat.

ALISON: Does this kind of thing happen often?

BECKY: Not often, but the prop sometimes gets fouled up.

LEE: I don't want to worry anyone, but I think the wind is getting up.

JASON: So's the sea. Look at those waves.

MRS. JOHNSON: Ouch! I'm wet. That wave splashed all over me.

MR. ALEXANDER: Don't worry, Mrs. Johnson. The rougher the sea, the more chance we have of freeing the rudder.

MRS. JOHNSON: Can't we go home, please?

JASON: We can't get back to port till the rudder's free, Mum.

MR. ALEXANDER: Take a look overboard, Lee. You might be able to see what's fouling the rudder.

LEE: O.K. I'll take a look.

BECKY: I'll get the boat-hook ready.

LEE: Stop fussing, Becky. I won't fall . . . help!

MRS. JOHNSON: He's fallen in!

MR. ALEXANDER: Where's the boat-hook?

BECKY: Here it is, Dad.

MR. ALEXANDER: Hang on, Lee.

ALISON: Thank heavens he's wearing his life-jacket. But Mr. Alexander isn't.

JASON: Quick, pass me that rope and I'll tie it round Mr. Alexander.

MR. ALEXANDER: Pull yourself in lad, hand over hand.

JASON: That's the line fixed.

MR. ALEXANDER: Take my hand Lee. Help! I'm slipping!

JASON: Don't worry, the line will hold you.

LEE: Ugh!

BECKY: Are you all right?

LEE: I'm wet.

MR. ALEXANDER: Did you see anything?

LEE: Yes. Water. Lots and lots of water.

MR. ALEXANDER: This is no time to be funny.

LEE: Of course I didn't see anything, Dad. I was trying to keep alive.

MR. ALEXANDER: Sorry, son. You did your best.

MRS. JOHNSON: Poor boy. Have you got a dry blanket?

MR. ALEXANDER: Of course not, woman. What do you think this is? A luxury liner?

MRS. JOHNSON: There's no need for you to talk to me like that.

BECKY: Come on, Dad. Try and get the steering going.

MR. ALEXANDER: I can't understand why it's not freed itself yet.

LEE: Maybe it's not fouled up. Maybe it's snapped.

MR. ALEXANDER: Impossible. Wait a minute – I think I can feel it coming free now.

MRS. JOHNSON: Thank goodness for that. I don't think I can stand much more of this.

MR. ALEXANDER: There we are. Going about now!

JASON: Look out for that big wave.

ALISON: Help! Now we're all soaking wet.

MR. ALEXANDER: Start baling! We're awash!

LEE: What with? We don't have any balers.

MR. ALEXANDER: Use anything you can lay your hands on.

ALISON: There are some plastic cups here.

MR. ALEXANDER: That'll do. If we take on any more water, we'll be in trouble.

MRS. JOHNSON: Oh no! We're going to sink!

MR. ALEXANDER: Shut up and bale.

MRS. JOHNSON: How dare you speak to me like that? I'm never coming on your boat again.

MR. ALEXANDER: Is that a promise?

BECKY: If we don't get on with the baling, there won't be a boat to come on.

LEE: How bad is it, Dad?

MR. ALEXANDER: Just keep baling and praying.

JASON: It's coming in faster than we can get it out.

MR. ALEXANDER: Keep at it, lad. There's Colnemouth ahead. Not far now.

MRS. JOHNSON: Thank heavens for that.

BECKY: Are you sure that's Colnemouth?

MR. ALEXANDER: Of course I'm sure.

ALISON: I don't think it is. That's a hill there on the left and Colnemouth hasn't got any hills near it.

MRS. JOHNSON: Why bother where it is, as long as it's dry land?

MR. ALEXANDER: It's got to be Colnemouth.

JASON: Haven't you got a chart?

BECKY: Dad's not very good on charts.

MRS. JOHNSON: We're lost. We'll be wrecked on the reef.

ALISON: We won't be wrecked. We'll just end up at the wrong harbour.

MR. ALEXANDER: Well, that's it.

BECKY: What's happened?

MR. ALEXANDER: Engine's packed up.

LEE: Don't say the prop's fouled?

MR. ALEXANDER: No. We've run out of petrol.

MRS. JOHNSON: Fire the distress rockets and call out the lifeguard!

MR. ALEXANDER: We don't have any distress rockets.

NOW YOU CAN FINISH THE PLAY YOURSELVES

Here are some ideas for finishing the play:

1. Are they going to be rescued?
2. Is there some way they can get the boat back to the harbour?
3. Remember, they are at the wrong harbour — are there rocks that they don't know about?
4. What would be the safest thing for them to do? (They don't have enough life-belts.)

THE TRAIN

*

Characters

MR. STEVENS
MRS. STEVENS
IAN STEVENS
FOREIGN LADY
NUN
LADY WITH DOG
POLICEMAN
GUARD
MANNISH LADY

The Train

The play takes place in the compartment of a train

MRS. STEVENS: Come along, Ian. Sit down there.

IAN: Next to the lady with the dog?

MRS. STEVENS: That's right.

IAN: I don't like the look of that dog.

LADY WITH DOG: My little Topsy Wopsy wouldn't hurt a fly.

IAN: She might not hurt flies, but how do I know that she won't hurt me?

LADY WITH DOG: What a nasty little boy. Isn't he a nasty little boy, Topsy Wopsy?

FOREIGN LADY: Ees thees the right train for London?

MRS. STEVENS: If it isn't, then we're on the wrong train.

FOREIGN LADY: Oh dear. Then we are on the wrong train.

NUN: No, this is the train for London.

FOREIGN LADY: Thank you, sister. I am a foreigner to this country and I do not know your customs.

IAN: Why has that lady got a black thing on her head?

MRS. STEVENS: She's a nun. And I've told you before. Don't make remarks about how other people look.

IAN: I wasn't making remarks. I asked a question. And what's a nun?

MRS. STEVENS: Sh. She'll hear you.

NUN: I don't mind you talking about me, young man. I'm someone who's decided to serve God.

IAN: Like a vicar?

NUN: That's right.

IAN: But why do you have to wear those clothes to do it?

MRS. STEVENS: Oh, Ian! I'm sorry, sister. He should know better.

NUN: That's all right. It's just a custom, Ian, just a custom. I could ask you why you wear trousers.

IAN: Because . . . well because . . . Oh, I see what you mean.

(Mannish Lady comes in.)

MANNISH LADY: Excuse me. Is this seat taken?

MRS STEVENS: No. The one in the middle is free.

MANNISH LADY: Thank goodness for that. I've been looking for a seat for ages.

IAN: Why has she got such a deep voice, Mum?

MRS. STEVENS: Oh, Ian, be quiet.

IAN: Well, why has she?

MRS. STEVENS: Some ladies do.

IAN: And why does she have such hairy legs?

MRS. STEVENS: Will you be quiet?

IAN: But why . . .

MRS. STEVENS: Ian, I'm getting cross. Just read your comic, please.

IAN: All right. Oooh! The dog's snuffling at my comic.

LADY WITH DOG: Now then, Topsy Wopsy. Keep away from the little boy.

IAN: That's all right. I don't mind.

LADY WITH DOG: You may not mind. But I do. Goodness knows what my little Topsy Wopsy might pick up on a railway train.

IAN: Can I have something to eat, Mum?

MRS. STEVENS: Here's a sweet.

IAN: Thanks Mum. Hey! The dog's pinched my sweet.

LADY WITH DOG: Naughty little Topsy Wopsy. Mustn't eat sweeties. Bad for little doggie toothie pegs.

(Policeman comes in.)

POLICEMAN: Sorry to disturb you, ladies. But have you seen a man – about thirty-ish? Medium build. Fair hair.

MRS. STEVENS: We're all ladies here, officer. No men.

POLICEMAN: Thank you. But you will keep your eyes open, won't you?

(Policeman goes out.)

IAN: They must be looking for an escaped prisoner.

MRS. STEVENS: They won't find him in here.

FOREIGN LADY: What did the policeman say? I did not understand.

MANNISH LADY: He's looking for a man.

FOREIGN LADY: Why does he want a man?

MRS. STEVENS: We think the man has escaped from the police.

IAN: Mum, if the police are looking for a man, how can you be sure he's not here?

MRS. STEVENS: Don't be daft. There are only ladies here.

IAN: Are you sure?

MRS. STEVENS: Of course I'm sure.

IAN: How about the lady with the deep voice and the hairy legs?

MRS. STEVENS: Keep your voice down.

IAN: She could be a man in disguise. I think we ought to tell the police.

MRS. STEVENS: Ian! Where are you going?

MANNISH LADY: Not so fast, young man.

MRS. STEVENS: He's got a gun.

LADY WITH DOG: I think I'm going to faint.

FOREIGN LADY: Does this happen often on English trains?

MANNISH LADY: Funny, isn't it? You can never fool kids. Now sit quiet and no one will get hurt.

LADY WITH DOG: There are times when I wish that Topsy Wopsy was an Alsatian and not a Yorkshire Terrier.

MRS. STEVENS: What do you want us to do?

CROOK: Keep still, and just act nice and ordinary-like.

NUN: You don't mind if I read my breviary?

CROOK: Be my guest. But no funny stuff, mind.

NUN: A breviary is a religious book – not a comic.

LADY WITH DOG: I think Topsy Wopsy is going to be sick.

CROOK: And when we get to London, I'll take the boy.

IAN: Don't worry, Mum, I can look after myself.

MRS. STEVENS: What will you do with him?

CROOK: Nothing, lady. He's my cover to get out of the station. They're looking for a man – not a lady holding a kid's hand.

FOREIGN LADY: I do not think that I like England. I think I would like to go back to my own country.

IAN: Here's the policeman again.

CROOK: Remember, act natural.

(Policeman comes in.)

POLICEMAN: All right, ladies? Seen our man yet?

MRS. STEVENS: Oh no, officer. No. No, we haven't.

LADY WITH DOG: Oh no. Definitely not. We haven't seen any nasty man with a gun, have we, Topsy Wopsy?

POLICEMAN: Well, keep a look-out ladies. He's dangerous and he may . . . Hey! How did you know he had a gun?

NOW YOU CAN FINISH THE PLAY YOURSELVES

Here are some ideas for finishing the play:

1. Does the policeman realise which one is the crook?

2. Does the lady with the dog cover up her mistake and let the policeman go?

3. Does Ian try to capture the crook single-handed?

4. Or does the journey go quietly until they get to London?

HOLIDAY ADVENTURE

*

Characters

CLIVE COUSINS
MAGGIE COUSINS
MR. COUSINS
MRS. COUSINS

Holiday Adventure

The action takes place at a beach and on the cliffs behind

Scene I:

CLIVE: I'm bored. It's too cold to swim.

MAGGIE: I'm fed up with making sand castles.

CLIVE: We've dammed that stream so many times it's a wonder it still flows.

MRS. COUSINS: Stop moaning, you two. After all the money we've paid to come here.

MR. COUSINS: Quite right. In my young day we were never bored.

CLIVE: I don't suppose you were – working twelve hours a day in the factories.

MR. COUSINS: I'll thank you to watch your tongue, my lad.

MRS. COUSINS: Why don't you go for a nice walk on the cliffs?

CLIVE: Walks are boring.

MRS. COUSINS: Well, those kids over there have found something to do.

MR. COUSINS: That's right. Just look at them. Shinning up those cliffs like a couple of monkeys.

CLIVE: I bet you wouldn't let us do that.

MAGGIE: No, you wouldn't. You'd say it was dangerous and we might get stuck.

MRS. COUSINS: I expect you would, at that.

MR. COUSINS: I don't know, Edna. Those two kids look younger than ours.

MRS. COUSINS: All the same, they might get stuck, or even fall.

CLIVE: Of course we won't fall.

MAGGIE: Just look at them now. They're coming down.

CLIVE: Piece of cake. Child's play – that cliff.

MAGGIE: Go on, Mum, let us have a bash.

CLIVE: We can't come to any harm.

MAGGIE: If those kids can do it, so can we.

MRS. COUSINS: All right. But put your trainers on first.

CLIVE: Who needs trainers?

MAGGIE: We'll get a better grip with bare feet.

MR. COUSINS: Do as your mother says. Put your trainers on.

MAGGIE: No fear. Come on Clive. Race you to the cliff.

(Clive and Maggie go off.)

MRS. COUSINS: There they go. I hope they'll be all right.

MR. COUSINS: Of course they'll be all right. If those kids could do it, so can ours.

MRS. COUSINS: I hope they remember about the tide. It'll be right up to the bottom of the cliffs in an hour.

MR. COUSINS: Don't fuss, Edna. They'll be back in a few minutes.

Scene II:

Up the cliff

CLIVE: Beat you!

MAGGIE: Only because I tripped.

CLIVE: Excuses! Excuses!

MAGGIE: Come on, then. Are we climbing up this thing or not?

CLIVE: Lead on. If you think you can find a way. I'll take over when you get stuck.

MAGGIE: This is easy. There are lots of handholds.

CLIVE: And footholds. Whoops! Nearly slipped.

MAGGIE: Be careful. Mum'll never forgive you if you break your leg.

CLIVE: I don't know. I've always wanted to go for a ride in an ambulance with the lights flashing and things going *bee bah*!

MAGGIE: Oh, shut up and climb.

CLIVE: Upwards ever upwards.

MAGGIE: I can't find another ledge.

CLIVE: Of course you can.

MAGGIE: No, I can't. Look it's sheer rock from now on. I can't find a place to put a finger.

CLIVE: Let me see. Why don't you go out to the left a bit?

MAGGIE: Sheer rock.

CLIVE: To the right, then?

MAGGIE: You're on the right.

CLIVE: So I am. Let's see. Here we are. There's a little bump up here.

MAGGIE: Be careful.

CLIVE: Stop fussing. You sound just like Mum.

MAGGIE: Have you got enough to hold on to?

CLIVE: Yes, of course. Here I go.

MAGGIE: I'll follow you.

CLIVE: Loads of room up here on this ledge.

MAGGIE: What a view!

CLIVE: There's Mum and Dad. Let's wave.

MAGGIE: We've climbed quite a way.

CLIVE: I'm glad we won't have to climb down.

MAGGIE: I don't think I could.

CLIVE: Those kids did it, but it's more difficult than it looks.

MAGGIE: Well, how are we going to get down?

CLIVE: We'll climb right up to the top and come down the cliff path.

MAGGIE: But the cliff doesn't end at the path. There's all that heather to cross.

CLIVE: It won't be hard to cross the heather.

MAGGIE: In bare feet?

CLIVE: Now you come to mention it . . . I hadn't thought of that.

MAGGIE: My feet hurt already.

CLIVE: And so do my legs. Come on, let's get moving.

MAGGIE: I don't see any more handholds.

CLIVE: There must be some.

MAGGIE: I don't see any.

CLIVE: You're right – it's sheer rock.

MAGGIE: What'll we do?

CLIVE: Climb back down.

MAGGIE: But we just said we couldn't.

CLIVE: Well, we've got to. Come on.

MAGGIE: I can't, I'm scared.

CLIVE: Look there's nothing to it. Just keep your back to the rock and – ooooh!

MAGGIE: Hang on. I've got you.

CLIVE: That was a narrow squeak.

MAGGIE: "Nothing to it," he says, and then nearly falls off. I'm not moving.

CLIVE: But you'll have to move.

MAGGIE: You can do what you like. It was a stupid idea – we should never have tried to climb these cliffs and I'm staying *here*.

CLIVE: You can't stay here.

MAGGIE: I'm stuck and I'm not moving until we get some help.

CLIVE: How can we get help?

MAGGIE: Take off your shirt and wave it.

CLIVE: I can't do that. I need both hands to hang on to the rock.

MAGGIE: If you don't, we'll be here all night.

CLIVE: And I've just remembered. The tide!

MAGGIE: Well, get your tee shirt off.

CLIVE: O.K. Here goes.

MAGGIE: Good lad.

CLIVE: But *(pant)* why *my (pant)* tee shirt?

MAGGIE: I don't want to catch cold.

CLIVE: Typical. I've got to risk my neck because you don't want to catch cold.

MAGGIE: Just get on with it.

CLIVE: Off with it, you mean.

MAGGIE: Now wave it about.

CLIVE: What if nobody sees it?

MAGGIE: Of course someone will see it. Get waving.

CLIVE: Dad's waving back. He thinks we're doing it for fun.

MAGGIE: Look! Mum's waving a towel.

CLIVE: And Dad's coming over here.

MAGGIE: Don't say he's going to try to rescue us!

CLIVE: He'll never make it. He gets out of breath climbing the stairs.

MAGGIE: Here he is.

MR. COUSINS *(From below)*: Hold on, kids. I'm coming.

CLIVE: Even if he does get up here, how is he going to get us down?

MAGGIE: Maybe he's got a rope.

CLIVE: I don't see any rope. Where would he have got a rope from?

MR. COUSINS *(From below)*: Don't panic. I'll be with you in a minute.

CLIVE: We're O.K., Dad. We just can't get down.

MR. COUSINS *(From below)*: I'll have you out of there in a jiffy.

MAGGIE: I hope so. My legs are stiff.

MR. COUSINS: Right. Here we are. What's the problem?

MAGGIE: We can't go any higher and we're scared to come down.

MR. COUSINS: Right then. I think the easiest thing will be for me to help you to go up.

CLIVE: O.K., Dad. You find the handholds.

MR. COUSINS: No problem. Let's just see. It may look sheer, but there's always a few cracks and . . .

MAGGIE: And?

MR. COUSINS: There don't seem to be any.

CLIVE: That's what we found.

MR. COUSINS: No problem. We'll just go down the way we came.

MAGGIE: But we're scared.

MR. COUSINS: Nothing to it. You just face the rock and find the footholds like this . . . Oooooh!

CLIVE: Not so easy, is it, Dad?.

MR. COUSINS: No it isn't. Well there's only one thing for it.

MAGGIE: What's that, Dad?

MR. COUSINS: Get waving that tee shirt again. We're all stuck.

NOW YOU CAN FINISH THE PLAY YOURSELVES

Here are some ideas for finishing the play:

1. Who comes to rescue them: the coastguards, a helicopter or another set of holidaymakers?
2 How do they all react to the situation?
3 Do they try again to climb out of danger?
4 What does Mrs. Cousins have to say once they are rescued?

THE GHOST OF
NEWTON CASTLE

*

Characters

AUNT JANE
UNCLE ALEX
PETER
SALLY
GUIDE
JOE

The Ghost of Newton Castle

The action of the play takes place in Newton Castle dungeon

PETER: Come on, Uncle Alex. There's nothing to be scared of.

UNCLE ALEX: I don't know. Those stories might be true.

SALLY: Even if there were a ghost, whoever heard of a ghost hurting people?

AUNT JANE: I don't like the look of those dungeons at all. Let's not go.

(Guide comes in.)

GUIDE: Good afternoon. Thinking of going into the dungeons, are you?

PETER: Yes, we are.

GUIDE: I wouldn't do that if I were you.

SALLY: Why not? Aren't they safe?

GUIDE: They're safe enough but . . .

UNCLE ALEX: But what?

GUIDE: The White Lady walks through there.

PETER: What White Lady?

GUIDE: The White Lady of Newton Castle, of course.

SALLY: Who was she?

GUIDE: The story goes that she was shut up here and died of hunger.

UNCLE ALEX: What was she shut up for?

GUIDE: Something to do with a will, I think. She would have got the castle and all its lands if she had lived to be twenty-one.

SALLY: But her wicked stepfather locked her up in the dungeon.

GUIDE: No, it was her uncle. The story goes that *he* did the dirty deed.

AUNT JANE: So now she haunts the dungeons.

GUIDE: That's right. So I wouldn't go down there if I were you.

PETER: It's all nonsense.

SALLY: I don't believe a word of it. Do you Uncle Alex?

UNCLE ALEX: I don't know. I'm not so sure.

AUNT JANE: I don't want to go into those dungeons.

PETER: Oh come on, don't be such stick-in-the-muds.

GUIDE: Don't say I didn't warn you.

(Guide goes out.)

AUNT JANE: I'm not coming.

UNCLE ALEX: Come on, Jane, where's your spirit of adventure?

AUNT JANE: I never had one.

PETER: Please, Aunt Jane. It won't be the same if you don't come.

AUNT JANE: All right. But if I see any ghosts, I'm off.

SALLY: Good for you, Aunt Jane. Come on.

UNCLE ALEX: Bit dark in here, isn't it?

PETER: Look at those chains. People must have lain forgotten there for years.

SALLY: It's a bit damp and smelly.

AUNT JANE: Not much to see really, is there?

UNCLE ALEX: I expect that's why they make up the ghost story bit.

PETER: To make you think you're getting your money's worth.

SALLY: What's that coming along the passageway?

AUNT JANE: It's a ghost! I'm off.

(Aunt Jane runs out.)

UNCLE ALEX: Come back, Jane. It's not a ghost. It's only . . .

SALLY: A ghost.

PETER: The White Lady!

UNCLE ALEX: Come on, kids, let's get out of here.

PETER: That's funny. She's gone.

SALLY: Right into that room.

PETER: She went through the door, too – not through the wall.

UNCLE ALEX: Are you coming or are you not?

SALLY: I'd like to stay and have another look.

PETER: So would I.

UNCLE ALEX: On your head be it. I need a brandy. Meet us in the café in twenty minutes.

(Uncle Alex goes out.)

PETER: All right, Uncle Alex, we'll be there.

SALLY: See you in twenty minutes!

PETER: Now we can really have a good look round.

SALLY: What do you expect to find?

PETER: I'm not sure, but I don't think we saw a ghost.

SALLY: Neither do I. It was a white figure, but it was rather solid, for a ghost.

PETER: You couldn't see through it, could you? Let's have a good look in the dungeon that it went into.

SALLY: Watch out. Someone's coming.

PETER: Uncle Alex, I expect, worried about us.

SALLY: No it's not. Let's hide.

(Guide and Joe come in.)

JOE: I still say, Bert — I don't like the idea.

GUIDE: Don't worry, Joe. It's working like a charm. You should have seen the couple that were down here just now.

JOE: You mean I really scared them?

GUIDE: Scared them? They're sitting in the café looking as white as ghosts themselves.

JOE: All the same, we can't run the risk for too long.

GUIDE: Don't worry, Joe. You make a marvellous ghost.

JOE: It's only a matter of time before someone finds me out.

GUIDE: Look, forget it. Leave the worrying to me. Let's check the loot.

JOE: That's another thing. The castle isn't closed yet. How do we know that no one will come?

GUIDE: I think of everything, Joe. There's a sign on the dungeon door now – "Closed for Repairs". It's as safe as the Bank of England.

JOE: Don't say that. The Bank wasn't safe enough for this stuff.

GUIDE: Let's get on with the check.

JOE: Why do we have to check it?

GUIDE: If we're getting rid of the stuff, we have to know exactly what we're selling.

JOE: Not much light in here, is there?

GUIDE: Of course not. That's all part of the plan. I've got a torch.

JOE: All right. How many bags should there be?

GUIDE: Ten. Each one with its own little gems.

JOE: How are you going to fence the stuff?

GUIDE: Leave it to me, Joe. You're great with a jemmy and even better as a ghost, but when it comes to brains, that's my department.

JOE: O.K. As long as I get my cut. And I don't catch my death of cold in this freezing dungeon.

GUIDE: There. That's a good enough sample of the goods for the fence. Let's hide this stuff away and clear off.

JOE: Right. Back it goes. Nice and safe.

GUIDE: And we'll leave the dungeon locked up for the night.

(Joe and Guide go out.)

PETER: Well, what do you think of that?

SALLY: I told you there wasn't a ghost.

PETER: Not only that. But they've got a load of loot hidden here.

SALLY: Do you also realise that we're locked in?

PETER: Of course I do, and we've got to get out. We'll have to tell the police about all this.

SALLY: There might be a reward.

PETER: Come on. Let's get out of here.

SALLY: But how? We're trapped!

PETER: No we're not. We can get out of that window up there.

SALLY: It's not too high up.

PETER: No it's not. If you stand on my shoulders, you should be able to reach it.

SALLY: And leave you here!

PETER: Don't be silly. I'll be all right. You tell Uncle Alex what's happened. Then go to the police and they'll come and get me out.

SALLY: All right. Give me a hand to get up.

PETER: Here you are. Hang on to the wall.

SALLY: I am hanging on to the wall – for grim death.

PETER: Can you reach?

SALLY: Yes I can. It's only a slit.

(Guide and Joe come in)

GUIDE: Hello, hello, what have we here?

NOW YOU CAN FINISH THE PLAY YOURSELVES

Here are some ideas for finishing the play:

1 Does Sally get out?
2 What will the crooks do to Peter?
3 Do the aunt and uncle take any action?
4 Do the thieves get caught or do they get away?

THE AIRFIELD MYSTERY

*

Characters

SAMANTHA
ERROL
SANJIT
JENNY
MAX
KARL

The Airfield Mystery

Scene I

A country road

SAMANTHA: I'm tired. I can't go any further without a rest.

JENNY: Same here. I ache all over. And for goodness sake, switch off that radio.

ERROL: I like to have music while I pedal.

SAMANTHA: And I like to have peace while I rest.

SANJIT: All right, girls – stop nagging. The reason you're not fit is that you don't get enough exercise.

SAMANTHA: We *are* fit. It's the bikes that are unfit. Look at mine. Noah rode it round the ark.

JENNY: We're not like you – *we* haven't got gears. Those hills were no joke without gears.

ERROL: You break my heart. O.K. we'll have a rest. Let's have a look at the map.

SANJIT: We don't need a map. I know where we are.

SAMANTHA: So do I – we're lost in the middle of nowhere.

JENNY: I can see the headlines now – four skeletons found by rusting bikes.

SAMANTHA: Mine's rusty enough now. Where do you think we are, then, clever clogs?

SANJIT: Little Gintle.

ERROL: Little what?

SANJIT: Little Gintle. It's a small airfield. My Dad sometimes comes gliding here.

SAMANTHA: I don't see any aeroplanes.

SANJIT: There aren't any. It's only used at the weekends. Look, there's the windsock over there.

ERROL: He's right, you know. I suppose it is flat enough for an airfield.

SANJIT: Those sheds over there are where they keep the gliders.

JENNY: Can we go and have a look?

ERROL: I thought you were too tired to move.

SAMANTHA: We're too tired to pedal any more. But this might be interesting.

SANJIT: All right. Come on. Leave the bikes against the wall here.

ERROL: It doesn't look very interesting. Just a couple of tatty old sheds.

JENNY: It may not be interesting, but it's easier on the legs than cycling.

SAMANTHA: Shall we be able to get inside the sheds?

SANJIT: I doubt it. They should be locked and only the club secretary has a key.

ERROL: Not much point in going over, is there?

JENNY: Oh come on, Errol. Where's your sense of adventure?

ERROL: We're looking at sheds – not going big-game hunting.

SAMANTHA: What's that noise?

SANJIT: What noise? I can't hear anything.

JENNY: I can. It sounds like a lawn mower.

ERROL: What would a lawn mower be doing here?

SAMANTHA: Cutting the grass?

SANJIT: It's not a lawn mower, anyway. It's an aeroplane.

ERROL: What's he doing here?

JENNY: It looks as if he's coming in to land.

SAMANTHA: If he's not coming in to land, he's flying a bit too low for comfort.

SANJIT: He *is* landing. Look!

JENNY: Come on – let's have a closer look.

SANJIT: Don't get too close.

SAMANTHA: Of course not. We're not stupid.

ERROL: Do you recognise them, Sanjit?

SANJIT: Never seen either of them in my life before.

JENNY: Maybe they're up to no good.

SAMANTHA: They might be smugglers or bank robbers or something.

ERROL: Don't worry – they're probably dull businessmen.

SANJIT: Nothing exciting ever happens to me.

JENNY: Look. They're waving.

SANJIT: Maybe they want us to help.

ERROL: Perhaps they don't know where they are.

KARL: Hey, you kids. What are you doing here?

ERROL: Watching you.

MAX: Cut out the funny stuff. Clear off. This is private property.

SANJIT: I know. It's the property of Upthorne Gliding Club.

JENNY: His dad's a member.

KARL: Sorry, son. That's all right, then.

MAX: I don't like it. These kids being here.

KARL: Calm down, Max. Perhaps they can help us.

ERROL: Sure. What can we do?

KARL: We've got to put this aircraft in the hangar. Can you give us a push?

SANJIT: Of course.

KARL: Max, you stay with the kids and tell them what to do.

MAX: O.K. But I don't like it. You – go and open the hangar doors.

SANJIT: Where's the key?

MAX: Here. And open them as wide as you can.

JENNY: Listen to old bossy boots.

MAX: The rest of you, get behind the wings and push. You two girls on that side. The boy and me on this side.

JENNY: I don't know why they call them *light* aircraft. This one weighs a ton.

SAMANTHA: Maybe the pilot's left the brake on.

JENNY: Samantha, what do you think of these blokes?

SAMANTHA: I don't know. I don't think I like them.

JENNY: Neither do I. I think they're up to something.

MAX: You girls – cut the chatter and push.

JENNY: We *are* pushing.

SAMANTHA: As hard as we can.

MAX: I'll give you a hand.

ERROL: What about me? I can't push this thing on my own.

MAX: We're nearly there. Be careful going through the doors.

ERROL: There's a car in here.

SANJIT: That's Mr. Hedges' car. He's the airfield manager.

KARL: O.K. Well done, kids.

MAX: Have you got the bag, Karl?

KARL: Of course I have.

MAX: Good. It wouldn't do to forget that.

KARL: And now, if you children will go into the office, you will find a reward for all your hard work.

MAX: What are you talking about?

KARL: Don't spoil it for the children, Max. It's a surprise. After you, kids.

SANJIT: You go first, girls.

SAMANTHA: I wonder what it is?

JENNY: I hope it's something to eat.

ERROL: We'll soon find out.

SANJIT: It's Mr. Hedges. Bound and gagged!

ERROL: What's this?

(Door bangs.)

SAMANTHA: They've locked us in.

JENNY: That's right. I told you they were up to something.

NOW YOU CAN FINISH THE PLAY YOURSELVES

Here are some ideas for finishing the play:

1 Who are the two men and what are they up to?
2 Why is Mr. Hedges bound and gagged?
3 How do the children get out?
4 Do Max and Karl get away with it?

I KNOW WHERE I'M GOING

*

Characters

KAREN COX
GUY COX
MRS. HILDA COX
MR. TED COX
GROUND STEWARD
SECURITY MAN
STEWARDESS

I Know Where I'm Going

The action of the play is progressive: following the Cox family on their headlong rush to catch a plane, from an underground train, to the air terminal and then on to the plane

KAREN: Is this train never going to move?

MR. COX: It's all your fault, Hilda. We had plenty of time until you decided to buy a new dress.

MRS. COX: I didn't have anything to wear for the evening.

GUY: You've got a case full of dresses, Mum.

MR. COX: And if this train doesn't get a move on, you'll be wearing that new dress at home – not in Benidorm.

MRS. COX: How was I to know that the train would break down?

MR. COX: All right. I shouldn't have listened to you.

GUY: It's moving again.

MR. COX: And about time, too.

KAREN: Look, we're at the station.

MR. COX: Everybody out and run for it.

GUY: What's our flight number? We can shout that as we go.

MR. COX: I've got the ticket here – 968 I think.

MRS. COX: That's it. I'm sure it is.

MR. COX: Where do we go here? Terminal Two – straight ahead. Terminal One to the right and Terminal Three to the left.

KAREN: So it's right for us.

MR. COX: This way. Follow me.

GUY: But Dad, that's *left*.

MR. COX: No time to argue. This is the way. Follow me.

MRS. COX: Do as your dad says.

MR. COX: Come on, you kids. Keep going.

GUY: But Dad . . .

MRS. COX: Quiet, Guy. You heard what your dad said.

KAREN: But Mum . . .

MR. COX: Be quiet, we're nearly there. What gate for Flight 968?

GROUND STEWARD: Gate Nineteen. But you'd better hurry – they made the last call ages ago.

MR. COX: It's a good thing we checked the bags in before we went for your dress.

GUY: That's what I'm trying to say . . .

MRS. COX: Quiet, Guy. Keep your breath for running.

KAREN: Let's give up, Guy. They'll find out soon enough.

MR. COX: Fifteen . . . Seventeen . . . There it is. Gate Nineteen.

MRS. COX: It must be almost time for take-off.

KAREN: Maybe they won't let us on.

MR. COX: Of course they'll let us on. We've got tickets and boarding cards, haven't we?

MRS. COX: Gate Nineteen. At last. Look, they're still searching some people.

MR. COX: We've even time to get our breath back.

SECURITY MAN: Walk through the scanner, please.

MRS. COX: Certainly. Here's our hand luggage.

SECURITY MAN: What's this? I'll have to open it.

MRS. COX: Whatever for?

SECURITY MAN: We're getting a positive reaction from the scanner.

MR. COX: My wife's got nothing in there that she shouldn't have.

MRS. COX: There you are. Nothing.

SECURITY MAN: This is what's causing the trouble. Your alarm clock.

MRS. COX: Oh, dear! I didn't mean to put that in. You don't need an alarm clock on holiday, do you?

SECURITY MAN: On holiday, are you? Bit of a long way for a holiday, isn't it?

MR. COX: Lots of people go there for holidays.

SECURITY MAN: Yes. Plenty of sand. Ha! Ha! Better hurry up – or you won't get there at all.

MR. COX: Come on, everyone. Get a move on.

SECURITY MAN: Have a good trip.

MRS. COX: Is this our plane?

KAREN: It isn't a giraffe.

MR. COX: Of course it's our plane. What's wrong with it?

MRS. COX: It's a bit bigger than the ones we usually fly in.

GUY: Mum – haven't you heard of Jumbo jets?

MRS. COX: I thought they were only for people going on long trips.

MR. COX: Of course not. They use them a lot in the holiday season.

KAREN: Look, the stewardess is waving.

GUY: Show her our boarding cards.

STEWARDESS: Do hurry up. The captain has permission to taxi out.

MR. COX: We're coming as fast as we can.

STEWARDESS: Good. That's everyone on board now.

MRS. COX: We made it.

STEWARDESS: Find yourselves some seats and don't forget to fasten your seat belts!

MRS. COX: This is nice. Much roomier than the plane we were on last year.

KAREN: No wonder.

GUY: Shall we tell them?

KAREN: Don't bother. They'll find out soon enough. Let's enjoy it while we can.

MR. COX: Have you seen the other passengers?

MRS. COX: I haven't had time yet.

MR. COX: They're a rum-looking lot, and no mistake.

MRS. COX: What do you mean, Ted?

MR. COX: Well I know Benidorm's popular with the British — but this plane is full of Arabs.

MRS. COX: That's something new. I didn't see any Arabs there last year.

MR. COX: You'd think they'd had enough of sun and sand where they come from.

MRS. COX: But they won't have all the bars and things, will they? No vino and all that.

MR. COX: That'll be it. They're only going for the wine!

GUY: I thought Arabs didn't believe in drinking wine.

KAREN: We're at the end of the runway.

GUY: Ready to take off for where?

MRS. COX: Alicante, of course. You should know that by now.

GUY: Who knows? Maybe we'll end up somewhere quite different this year.

MRS. COX: I don't know what you're talking about, Guy.

KAREN: Maybe we'll be hi-jacked.

MR. COX: I wouldn't be surprised at anything that happens nowadays.

KAREN: Here we go. Hang on to your hats.

MRS. COX: It's very smooth in this big plane, isn't it, Ted?

MR. COX: Very smooth indeed. Very nice.

MRS. COX: Not like that awful old plane we were on last year.

MR. COX: This doesn't feel like flying at all, does it?

GUY: The sign's off now. We can unfasten our seat belts.

KAREN: Here comes the stewardess.

STEWARDESS: We will be serving lunch in a few minutes. Did you order anything special?

MR. COX: No, should we have?

STEWARDESS: Oh no. It's only if you want something different because of your religion.

MRS. COX: We'll just have what the others are having, thank you.

STEWARDESS: Would you like something to drink, sir?

MR. COX: I'll have a light ale, thank you. What'll you have, Hilda?

MRS. COX: Sweet sherry, please.

MR. COX: And a couple of lemonades for the kids.

STEWARDESS: Thank you, sir.

MRS COX: This is nice, I must say. Comfy seats. Waited on hand and foot. I really feel as if I'm on holiday.

CAPTAIN'S VOICE: This is your captain speaking. On behalf of my crew I should like to welcome you aboard Flight BA 968.

The weather is fine and the estimated time of arrival in Kuwait . . .

MR. COX: Kuwait! He's on the wrong plane!

MRS. COX: We're going to Alicante. Not Kuwait.

STEWARDESS: Is something the matter?

MR. COX: I'll say something's the matter. We're booked to Alicante and this bloke says we're going to Kuwait.

STEWARDESS: So we are. This is Flight BA 968 to Kuwait. Let me see your tickets.

MR. COX: Here they are. Look BA . . . Oh no . . .

STEWARDESS: BA 896 – to Alicante!

MRS. COX: Ted – you looked at them upside down! Ted, Ted, what shall we do?

NOW YOU CAN FINISH THE PLAY YOURSELVES

Here are some ideas for finishing the play:

1 What happens when they get to Kuwait?
2 Will they have to pay their fares home?
3 Does some rich Arab offer to help them out?
4 Does something unexpected happen – a hi-jacking for example?